THE OPENING SALES

The Selling Techniques

By

Max Police

© Copyright 2020 by (Max Police) - All rights reserved.

This document is geared towards providing exact and reliable information in regards to the topic and issue covered. The publication is sold with the idea that the publisher is not required to render accounting, officially permitted, or otherwise, qualified services. If advice is necessary, legal or professional, a practiced individual in the profession should be ordered.

- From a Declaration of Principles which was accepted and approved equally by a Committee of the American Bar Association and a Committee of Publishers and Associations.

In no way is it legal to reproduce, duplicate, or transmit any part of this document in either electronic means or in printed format. Recording of this publication is strictly prohibited and any storage of this document is not allowed unless with written permission from the publisher. All rights reserved.

The information provided herein is stated to be truthful and consistent, in that any liability, in terms of inattention or otherwise, by any usage or abuse of any policies, processes, or directions contained within is the solitary and utter responsibility of the recipient reader. Under no circumstances will any legal responsibility or blame be held against the publisher for any reparation, damages, or monetary loss due to the information herein, either directly or indirectly.

Respective authors own all copyrights not held by the publisher.

The information herein is offered for informational purposes solely, and is universal as so. The presentation of the information is without contract or any type of guarantee assurance.

The trademarks that are used are without any consent, and the publication of the trademark is without permission or backing by the trademark owner. All trademarks and brands within this book are for clarifying purposes only and are the owned by the owners themselves, not affiliated with this document.

Table of contents

INTRODUCTION 4

CHAPTER 1: GETTING STARTED WITH THE SELLING TECHNIQUES 9

1.1 Sales Prospecting Techniques 9

1.2 Selling Techniques that Create Value 10

1.3 Methods for Phone Selling? 12

1.4 How may I improve my selling procedures 14

1.5 Step by Step instructions to offer to existing clients 15

1.6 Strategies that don't work 17

1.7 Plan Your Process (Marketing and Sales) 18

CHAPTER 2: SALES ALGORITHM 28

2.1 Sales Process 28

2.2 Sales Process Steps 30

2.3 The most effective method to Improve Your Sales Process 33

2.4 Model on How to Map the Sales Process 37

2.5 Sales Process Common Mistakes 38

2.6 Common Sense Matters a Lot 40

2.7 Keep Moving Forward 43

CONCLUSION 46

Introduction

Before you get the telephone to settle on a sales decision to a chief, I'd prefer to propose you recollect the accompanying genuine story:

A couple of months prior, one of my salespeople, Daniel, had some vehicle issues, so I offered to give him a ride to work. Not having any desire to leave behind the occasion to do somewhat one-on-one pretending, I proposed we go over some arrangement setting telephone abilities. I've had a long-standing, very much demonstrated measurement that you have only eight seconds to catch a chief's eye at whatever point they get their telephone. Daniel was somewhat incredulous about my eight-second norm. He took a gander at me and stated, "Chief, eight seconds is too short a timeframe! That is not really sufficient opportunity to take a full breath, not to mention offer a significant opening expression."

We turned out to be holding up at a red light when he said this. As the light turned green, I kept my foot on the brake and began tallying: "1,000 one, 1,000 two...." People began sounding. When I got to "1,000 four," Daniel was imploring me to get going. When we hit the 6th second, the person behind us was beginning to escape his vehicle, and Daniel was searching for a put under the wood planks to stow away. When I was at long last hit eight, the convergence was an orchestra of sounding horns, "pointing fingers," and yelling mouths. I hit the gas.

Daniel's never addressed me again on how long eight seconds truly is or whether you can affect that timeframe.

On the off chance that you've been perusing my sections, you comprehend what spurs individuals to get; you know the essential points of interest about your item, administration, or arrangement; and you have a smart thought about the techniques available to you for reaching individuals who may give you new business. When you end up preparing to get the telephone to call a leader, what do you say?

I will expect that your objective for getting the telephone is to grow new business. I'm additionally going to expect that:

- You've chosen to utilize the telephone to do this, either by methods for a subsequent approach, a composed correspondence or as your first contact with the objective business.
- Your point is to get an arrangement or make the subsequent stage with a top leader who is the individual who can purchase whatever it is you're selling.

You have three primary objectives concerning building up an initial articulation that works. You need to:

1. Make it sound conversational.
2. Deliver it with certainty.
3. Get a significant interference - one that will place your possibility in charge at the earliest opportunity.

Five Key Opening Statement Components

You're getting the telephone to call your possibility. For the present moment, we should accept you to break through to the Chief. (You should peruse a month ago's the segment to adapt precisely how to move beyond the watchmen.) Here are the five essential fixings your initial proclamation needs to contain:

1. An Introduction

Typically, when a leader (or any other individual) gets a direct line, they state their name: "This is Jane Smith," or "Jane Smith speaking." Your initial step will be to rehash this current individual's name. Save things formal for the present - use Mr. or, on the other hand, Ms., at that point, the contact's last name.

- Prospect: This is Jane Smith.
- You: Ms. Smith?
- Prospect: Yes.

This initial step will win you Ms. Smith's full focus. Whatever she was doing before you say her name, she's presently quit doing. She's focusing on you, and that is something to be thankful for!

What most salespeople do now-- notwithstanding abundant and unendingly rehashed proof that they shouldn't-- states something like this: "Hey, Ms. Smith. This is Will Perish, with the ABC Insurance Company." Unless your name is, state, James Bond, or your organization association is, state, the Prize Disbursement Division of Publishers Clearing House, I can let you know precisely what will occur next in by far most of such calls: The possibility will react to this reckless "verbal handshake" by blocking out, requesting that you send composed data, imagining the structure just burst into flames, or in any case separating from the call. You'll have just been on the line about a second and a half, and you'll be finished.

2. The Pleasantry

Here's an elective arrangement. What I'm going to reveal to you will negate what you've been instructed. Do it in any case.

At the point when Jane Smith says, "Yes," you will react with something positive and energetic, something that doesn't straightforwardly distinguish you, your organization, or the item or administration you, in the end, need to examine. It's too soon in the relationship for you to pass along that sort of data. Instead, you will utilize merriment, for example, one of these:

- "It's an honor to at last talk with you!"
- "Thanks for getting the telephone!"
- "Thanks for accepting my call."
- "Your time is significant. Let me quit wasting time."

Get the thought? All of these merriments will improve work for you, then basically chipping in your name and friends association at the beginning of the discussion. Or, on the other hand, saying something faltering like "How's it hanging with you?" or "Do you have a moment?"

3. The Hook

Following your merriment, you will get the individual's consideration by utilizing a snare that is keyed straightforwardly to something prone to hold any importance with this possibility.

"We've helped (three of the best five gadget partnerships lessen overhead expenses by twelve percent this quarter-- and they did it without laying off staff or relinquishing item quality)."

Presently there's an absolute advantage if, at any point, there was one! Keep your snare engaged, and only a couple of sentences long, and you can't turn out badly.

The Interruption. Usually, here's the place you'll get hindered if your snare is managing its responsibility. Your possibility is probably going to cut in and state something along the lines of one of these announcements:

- "This sounds intriguing - reveal to me about it."
- "I haven't known about this previously. However, I should let it be known sounds dubiously intriguing."
- "I have positively no intrigue."

(Try not to stress. You'll be figuring out how to manage any not significant breaks in the following month's section.)

As I stated, you'll more likely than not get hindered by this point. However, you have to wrap up building up your initial explanation for the fulfillment, so you realize what to state in those situations where you don't get hindered now.

4. Naming Names

THE OPENING SALES

Whenever you've shared your snare, the other individual knows the purpose behind your call- - the real truth out in the open. This is simply the ideal chance to distinguish, and if you like, your association. In the event that you decide to recognize the name of your business, give it a concise "business." What you state will fit in one sentence. It should seem like this:

> "This is Will, Will Prosper, with ABC Insurance Company- - the most focused organization in the protection business today."

5. Your Ending Question

You will lose your initial explanation with a completion question that joins some component of time on the off chance that you don't get hindered by this point. Attempt one of these:

- "Ms. Smith, does this touch on issues that are of worry to you this (month/year/quarter)?"
- "Are you needing to achieve something like this before the finish of this (quarter/year)?"
- "Is this something you'd prefer to investigate further?"
- "Who in your group would you like for me to proceed with this discussion with among now and the finish of this business (day/week)?"

Assembling It All

Here's a case of an initial proclamation that works. Yours shouldn't sound precisely like this one, yet it ought to be about this long, and it should, similar to what follows, hit all the bases you've been finding out about.

- Prospect: "This is Jane Smith."
- You: "Ms. Smith?"
- Prospect: "Yes...."
- You: "(Pleasantry) It was a delight to peruse that your organization has effectively ventured into the European commercial center. By the way. (Hook) after examining another customer's activity, we recommended a thought that gave income additions of more than $25,000 every year. The genuine shock is that we did this without taking the slightest bit of Acme's well-deserved capital. (Your Name) This is Will Prosper at Zenith. (Finishing Question) Acme's noteworthy outcomes might be difficult to copy. Yet, OK, be available to make the following stride among now and the first of the year?"

Once more, you shouldn't attempt just to embed your organization particulars into the content you see above. It would be best if you utilized all the thoughts in this article to create an initial proclamation that is remarkably yours, and that best fits the business you're pitching.

Besides, with regard to selling, there are endless methodologies you can take.

Truth be told, you can discover many various sales techniques being executed on similar sales group at most associations.

Does this sound like your sales group? Is it true that you are and your sales partners simply blindly going for it regarding your selling system?

Provided that this is true, you're in good company.

A huge number of salespeople out there have no clue about what technique works best for them.

They're taking a blind leap of faith consistently, without an away from of why they're doing what they're doing.

THE OPENING SALES

Chapter 1: Getting Started with the Selling Techniques

Who couldn't utilize an armory of powerful selling strategies? In the event that you genuinely need to improve how you sell, look no farther than this examination supported an assortment of the absolute best B2B deals procedures, just as four ineffectual (however mainstream) thoughts for how to sell.

1.1 Sales Prospecting Techniques

Catching your purchaser's eye and making way for more productive deals discussions is the way to compelling deals prospecting. Utilize these three deals prospecting strategies to construct your pipeline and have more profitable discussions with your possibilities.

Make your Customer; Hero

There's a huge group of examination about the psychological impacts of stories for propelling conduct change. Furthermore, in a selling setting, stories are an amazing method to delineate the estimation of your answer for your possibility.

Each story needs a saint—somebody you identify with as they defeat snags on their excursion toward joyfully ever after. Be that as it may, who's the saint of your story? On the off chance that it's your organization or your answer, you have to modify your story and make the client the legend.

A run of the mill legend's excursion resembles this:

1. The legend is a character who battles with an issue
2. The legend meets an astute tutor who comprehends their concern
3. This tutor gives the saint new understanding, gives an arrangement, and drives them to activity
4. Armed with recently discovered certainty and an arrangement, the legend faces their concern
5. The saint beats the issue, understands their latent capacity, and arrives at their objective

In your story, the client is the person who needs to make all the difference, not you. Your job is that of the guide. You're there to enable your clients to perceive what has changed in their reality and how they can adjust to all the more likely to endure and flourish.

Don't Over-Personalize your Campaigns

THE OPENING SALES

Most advertisers and sales reps accept the more customized your effort, the better your outcomes. However, you might be astounded to find that exceptionally customized effort isn't as compelling as less time-serious personalization.

In an ongoing B2B personalization study, we tried the viability of four distinctive email personalization techniques with 7000 possibilities to figure out which treatment worked best. We utilized four distinctive personalization conditions—the industry just, the organization just, industry + individual subtleties, and friends + individual subtleties.

The outcomes? While open rates were higher when utilizing more close to home subtleties, the inverse was valid for navigating. Customizing by industry (without individual subtleties) restored a 24 percent higher active clicking factor than the organization + individual subtleties treatment.

Individuals may at first open an email that seems to talk straightforwardly to them. However, they'll feel let down when they find it's just a cunning trick to catch their eye. Then again, when you share a tale about how a comparative organization battled and fathomed a typical industry concern, your possibility is better ready to extend themselves into the story. They may even be anxious to discover what occurred straightaway.

Use "You" stating, not "We" expressing

It appears to be good-natured and intrinsically intelligent: Show your clients you comprehend their reality by situating yourself as an individual from their clan, planning to build up a collective encounter. "We" suggest the provider and the purchaser are "in it together." The issue is, the point at which you utilize this sort of we-expressing, you're really harming your capacity to move your possibility to make a move.

Corporate Visions ran two investigations to test the viability of you-expressing versus we-stating. The examinations found that you-stating is exponentially more viable at moving possibilities to assume individual liability and feel like they should make a move. You-expressing forces your possibility to scrutinize their business, as usual, paints an attainable purchasing vision, and holds your possibility's consideration such that isolates your message from the opposition.

In this way, whenever you're conversing with a likely purchaser, use you-stating. It's a little change. However, it has a major effect.

1.2 Selling Techniques that Create Value

Utilize these four offering methods to show your possibilities why they have to change their circumstance and convince them to pick you over your opposition.

Challenge your possibility's business as usual

Numerous salesmen see the business cycle as direct. Eventually, it has an end—the possibility will pick possibly you or your rival. The truth is that those aren't the main two endpoints. There's another choice—no choice—which is picked very regularly.

Studies show that 60% of the pipeline arrangements are lost to "no choice" as opposed to contenders in any event. That is a direct result of something many refer to as Status Quo Bias—your possibility's regular repugnance for accomplishing something other than what's expected than what they're doing today. It's simply by disturbing their business as usual that you can convince your possibilities that their present circumstance is hazardous and unreasonable.

Remember, in any case, that this discussion is regarding why your purchaser needs to change. It's not tied in with presenting your answers' highlights and advantages. Now, center around making the criticalness to change by setting up that your possibility's the norm circumstance is keeping them from arriving at their most significant business objectives.

Introduce Unconsidered Needs

Again and again, salesmen base their informing on the requirements possibilities reveal to you they have. At the point when you do that, you're at that point slanted to interface those distinguished needs to the particular capacities that react to those necessities—in the standard "arrangement selling" design.

The issue is, you wind up conveying product messages that won't separate you from your rivals—since they're probably building a comparable worth message in light of a similar arrangement of sources of info. What's more, on the grounds that each alternative sounds the equivalent, your possibilities become uncertain. To make the criticalness to change and defeat Status Quo Bias, you have to acquaint possibilities with Unconsidered Needs—neglected, undervalued, or yet obscure issues or botched chances that are keeping down their business.

Find your worth wedge

When you present your offer to possibilities, what amount cover is there between what you can give, and what your opposition can give? Most B2B salesmen concede that cover is 70% or higher. So instead of contending inside that "esteem equality region,"

THE OPENING SALES

center around what you can accomplish for the client that is not the same as what the opposition can do. This is called your Value Wedge.

Your Value Wedge must meet three significant models:

1. It's remarkable to you. This is a message that is totally unique in relation to your rivals.
2. It's imperative to the client. Offer some benefit by featuring holes in your possibility of doing things today and how your methodology will settle those issues.
3. It's faultless. Report evidence purposes of time when different organizations conquered comparable difficulties by embracing your proposed arrangement.

Also, when you make something that meets those three models, you have an offer that separates your answer from the opposition and conveys a genuine incentive to your possibility.

At the point when you interface your possibility's Unconsidered Needs to your separated qualities, you break liberated from esteem equality and ware informing to make the criticalness and separation expected to conquer your possibility's Status Quo Bias.

Tell convincing visual stories

"Passing by PowerPoint" is a typical method to portray the psyche desensitizing experience of enduring a long slide introduction loaded up with list items and clasp workmanship. However, most salesmen keep on swearing by this drained and unimaginative strategy for pitching.

However, research demonstrates that successful deals introductions need to go past the elite of projectiles. An exploration study we directed on utilizing visuals in B2B deals uncovered that straightforward, solid, hand-drawn visuals on a whiteboard outflanked two kinds of PowerPoint introductions in the zones of review, commitment, introduction quality, believability, and influence.

Deal's introductions ought to be a convincing visual story intended to exhibit your items and administrations and how they convey special worth. What's more, whether or not you utilize a whiteboard, a flip diagram, the rear of an envelope, or a tablet, utilizing visual stories is an amazing differentiator in serious and complex selling conditions.

1.3 Methods for Phone Selling?

The majority of the selling methodologies in this article are as yet powerful when you're selling via telephone, yet you can utilize these two explicit telephone deals strategies to support your influential effect and close more arrangements.

THE OPENING SALES

Tailor your directive for virtual deals

Numerous organizations are growing inside deals groups. Truth be told, most of the B2B salesmen we reviewed directly the greater part of their business brings in non-eye to eye conditions. Be that as it may, for all the potential cost reserve funds and profitability increases, inside deals can make commitment challenges because of the virtual hindrance among merchants and purchasers.

In an eye to eye meeting, you probably have your possibility's complete consideration. Be that as it may, via telephone or in a virtual gathering, there are a lot of other contending needs to occupy them. They may accept your call, yet except if they esteem what you're offering, they can without much of a stretch withdraw and keep working in different applications or browsing email while you're introducing your pitch.

That is the reason you have to tailor your conveyance for the particular circumstance they're in. They lack as expected, so come to the heart of the matter. They need to realize what you can offer, so acquaint Unconsidered Needs with catch their eye. Tell a convincing, relatable story and use visuals to hold their consideration while you show the estimation of your answer.

Encourage your possibility to partake

One undervalued, at this point, an exceptionally powerful strategy for telephone deals is utilizing intelligent visuals. As referenced before, there are clear advantages to utilizing hand-drawn visuals over the normal PowerPoint introduction. You can also apply this idea to telephone deals by getting your audience to partake somehow or another—regardless of whether by taking notes or by drawing a basic, concrete visual as coordinated.

Corporate Visions research uncovers that utilizing this way to deal with intelligent visual stories is imperative to draw in your crowd, expanding good mentalities toward your story, improving review, and making possibilities bound to meet with you.

Be cautioned. Fusing these narrating strategies into your virtual deals calls will request some conduct changes from salesmen. A considerable lot of the agents we worked with believed that utilizing intelligent visuals on deals calls made "an excess of rubbing" that would contrarily affect the call. In any case, subsequent to incorporating this method, they saw a prompt positive effect comparative with their past verbal-just methodology.

1.4 How may I improve my selling procedures

Persuading your clients to change their norm and pick you isn't sufficient to bring a close deal. Utilize these four deals shutting strategies to make direness, drive agreement among partners, and persuade your purchasers to make a move now.

Recount stories with contrast

Informing is tied in with recounting your organization's story in a way that draws in possibilities to your entryway and transforms them into clients. The test is that, in case you're similar to most organizations, you recount your story in a way that doesn't separate you much, if by any means. In any case, to make an amazing view of significant worth, you have to tell both the "previously" story and the "after" story—you have to tell client stories with contrast.

At the point when you tell client stories, don't be reluctant to connect information with feelings. The ideal approach to do that is to frequently discuss the individuals who were influenced by the difficult climate they were working in. At that point, talk about how their carries on with turned out to be better, simpler, more fun, or less unpleasant subsequent to utilizing your answer.

Feature the Danger

There's a longstanding legend that heads are carefully judicious in their dynamic, affected simply by the hard ROI story you can tell. However, that is just not the situation.

The examination showed the effect of Loss Aversion, an idea essential to Prospect Theory. Spearheaded by social therapists Amos Tversky and Daniel Kahneman, Prospect Theory expresses that people are 2-3 times bound to settle on a choice or face a challenge to evade a misfortune than to do likewise to accomplish an increase.

Ensure your worth

Purchasers today have all the force in deals dealings. They know it, thus do sales reps. As indicated by our exploration, 72 percent of B2B salesmen report that purchasers have developed all the more impressive in the course of the most recent quite a while. They have the certainty to request limits—and leave when they don't get them.

The issue is, numerous sales reps unconsciously make concessions all through the business cycle—esteem releases that make it harder to finalize the negotiation, which, thusly, makes it harder to ensure your edges during late-stage exchanges.

THE OPENING SALES

Worth releases occur as the purchaser attempts to pick up an agreement among different partners in the association. They flex their capacity and begin setting extra expectations for your time, your assets, and obviously, for limits. Furthermore, you may not know that it's occurring.

How would you secure your worth? While overseeing multi-party choices, consider who in the association thinks about the choice thinks about choice, and begins focusing on those partners in your discussions. At the point when you address the business sway for each key chief engaged with the buy, you can drive agreement quicker.

Influence urgent arrangements

As arrangements get progressively mind-boggling, late-stage arranging strategies become progressively superfluous. What's more, your capacity to make a beneficial result relies upon how deftly you explore crucial points in time of the business cycle — minutes that can possibly change the idea of your chance and recast the purchaser's view of your impact.

To assist you with doing this from a low-power position, think about the idea of Pivotal Agreements. The five sorts of Pivotal Agreements are esteem based trades that you can use to propel your arrangements while securing your resources.

The thought is to proactively choose what you need from the client to get the best ultimate result during the purchasing cycle. All in all, you catch the esteem and ensure your edges by executing a progression of Pivotal Agreements all through the purchasing cycle, as opposed to one thousand trade-offs toward the end.

1.5 Step by Step instructions to offer to existing clients

The deal isn't over in light of the fact that your possibility turns into a client. There's as yet sufficient occasion to drive development from client extension openings like recharges and upsells. Here are three examination sponsored deals strategies for offering to your current clients.

Protect your client's norm

At the point when you're connecting new possibilities, it bodes well to utilize a provocative testing approach that presents Unconsidered Needs, upsets their norm, and convinces them to pick you. As an untouchable, you need to outline their present circumstance as dangerous and hazardous and present your answer as a superior, more secure other option.

Be that as it may, when you're the insider, guarding your occupant position to existing clients, you frequently need to strengthen your worth and feature the reasons why you're as yet the most secure decision. Since you are your client's the norm, you can utilize their characteristic Status Quo Bias for your potential benefit during recharging and extension discussions.

To your current clients, you are their business as usual. Furthermore, research shows that utilizing a provocative testing message when you're attempting to reestablish or grow business with your clients will improve the probability that they'll look around by at any rate 10-16 percent.

Upsell by strengthening the relationship

Certain business discussions with your clients require more artfulness than others. For instance, development discussions walk a flimsy line between convincing your client to purchase more and persuading them to remain with your answer simultaneously. In the event that you succeed, you lay the preparation for a durable organization. Yet, in the event that you stagger, your association deteriorates, your income levels, and your client gets helpless against getting taken out by contenders.

With regards to winning upsell discussions, our exploration found that strengthening the enthusiastic parts of the client association was best in convincing clients to cause change to appear to be sheltered insofar as they're changing with you, not away from you.

In these circumstances, don't be reluctant to utilize enthusiastic language to incline toward the connection between you and your client's organization. At that point, influence that relationship to have a plain discussion about difficulties and openings befitting a drawn-out organization.

Purchasers are normally more slanted to stay with their business as usual than change to another arrangement. However, that doesn't mean you should underestimate your relationship. Your clients are continually being pitched by outside sellers who are anxious to win their business. Try not to give them a chance.

Realize how to apologize

Ideally, you could never need to apologize to your clients. However, administration disappointments are unavoidable. Also, misusing these vital minutes can put your client connections, maintenance, and future income in danger. However, it doesn't need to be that way.

Saying 'sorry' to your clients the correct way can recoup the relationship as well as really improve their dedication going ahead. Utilizing an idea called the Service Recovery Paradox as an establishment, our examination found that a particular conciliatory sentiment message system improved your client's odds of suggesting your item and purchasing more from you after an assistance disappointment.

1.6 Strategies that don't work

There's a great deal of "standard way of thinking" for how to sell out there that, as a general rule, doesn't really assist you with making the deal. Here are four exemplary go-to selling strategies that may, indeed, be harming your deals.

Try not to sale zero on selling benefits

Everybody realizes how to sell benefits and not highlights, isn't that so? Indeed, no. In the event that you start your client discussion with benefits, you're bouncing the firearm with regards to how most possibilities are taking a gander at their first communications with you and your organization.

Recollect that up to 60 percent of pipeline bargains are lost to business as usual. That implies that you have to figure out how to sell by setting up a purchasing vision—the case for why the possibility needs to change—before your answer's advantages will reverberate. That implies you have to viably stir things up and show how the possibility's reality can improve.

Try not to contend in a prepare off

At the point when you position yourself against your rivals, you're contending in a seller prepare off. It's a "spec war," and you may pick up the high ground with one component; however, the opposition meets your element and raises another.

All the while, you and your opposition are regularly having a fundamentally the same as exchange with the possibility, prompting the feared "no choice." Instead of conversing with the possibility of "why us," center rather around stirring things up by getting the possibility to consider "why change" and "why now," and show the really special estimation of your answer.

Try not to offer to personas

Numerous sales reps and advertisers use personas to create informing. Also, apparently, it appears to bode well: characterizing your possibility profile will empower you to create messages focused on that profile.

THE OPENING SALES

The issue is that personas are regularly characterized by who the possibility is – socioeconomics and practices. Yet, the need to change isn't driven by a persona. A possibility of comparative qualities with the persona isn't what makes them reexamine their present approach and think about your answer as another approach to tackle their issues.

Rather than creating messages dependent on personas, center around how to sell by persuading possibilities that the norm they are remaining on is "risky," at that point, give them how life is better with your answer.

1.7 Plan Your Process (Marketing and Sales)

"Business resembles battle in one regard. In the event that its stupendous methodology is right, quite a few strategic mistakes can be made, but the undertaking demonstrates fruitful."

Robert E. Wood - Executive and Brigadier General

To make genuine, enduring development for you and your organization, you have to make your own excellent methodology. Furthermore, that begins with a strong deals plan.

As very rich person financial specialist Warren Buffett puts it:

"Somebody's sitting in the shade today since somebody planted a tree quite a while past."

What is a business plan? Furthermore, for what reason would it be advisable for you to mind?

A business plan is "where, why, when, and how" that will direct you to hit your business objectives for the year.

A higher perspective aside, a business plan is a month-to-month estimate of the degree of deals you hope to accomplish and how you will arrive. It covers past deals, market concerns, your particular specialties, who your clients are, and how you will discover them, draw in with them, and offer to them.

Whenever done effectively, the correct deals plan layout enables you to invest considerably more energy in developing and building up your startup, as opposed to reacting to the everyday improvements in deals.

Equipped with the data you'll order inside your business plan, you can rapidly recognize any forthcoming issues, deals dry seasons, or openings — and afterward, take care of them. It might appear as though a ton of work to build up a business plan layout now, yet once you answer every one of these inquiries, you'll be in a spot to take your deals (and brand) to the following level.

To make things simpler, I will separate your business plan format into three particular areas:

- Sales determining and objective setting
- Market and client research
- Prospecting and associations

Each aspect of the business plan normally works itself into the following, beginning with your significant level objectives, at that point mulling over market factors, lastly taking a gander at who you know, and how to discover more possibilities to help hit your business objectives.

Set reasonable deals objectives in your business plan

Before we get into the cycle of how you will get your business this year, we have to discuss something greater: Goals.

Your business plan format needs an ultimate objective. You need a number — either deals or clients or whatever metric you pick — that will reveal to you whether what you've done has been a triumph. I've expounded on defining sensible deals objectives top to bottom previously; however, all that matters is figuring out what reasonably you can get dependent on the size of the market, your organization's objectives, and the experience and assets accessible to your business group.

Besides that, there are five different traps you ought to know about when defining your business objectives:

1. Wishful reasoning: You need your business to develop, so it's justifiable that you may be over-idealistic in building up your business plan. Start by seeing a year ago's figure and results. Is it safe to say that you were being practical? For new organizations, abstain from working out the degree of deals you should be suitable for and putting this as your figure. In brain science, we'd call this the affirmation inclination, but at the same time, it's an only straight-up terrible business.
2. Ignoring your own suspicions: Make sure your estimate depends on your suppositions about the market. In the event that you accept the market will decay, and you will lose some piece of the overall industry, it simply doesn't bode well to figure expanded deals.
3. Moving goal lines: For the most part, you need your gauge to be finished and concurred inside your business plan format on a set time span so you can get

onto the matter of, well, business. Abstain from making acclimations to the objectives sketched out in your business plan—regardless of whether you find you've been excessively hopeful or cynical in your business arranging. This report ought to be a benchmark to pass judgment on your prosperity or disappointment.

4. Not requesting a meeting: Your business group is down and dirty with you and presumably has the best information about your clients. Anyway, is there any valid reason why you wouldn't ask their conclusions, give them an opportunity to converse with their clients, and go to an understanding of the objectives that go into your business plan?
5. Not saving time for input: Having define your business objectives, you need somebody to come in and challenge it. Get an accomplished individual—a bookkeeper, senior sales rep, or qualified companion—to survey the whole record before taking it expansive and hardening your business plan.

Regardless of anything else, recollect that when you're building up your business plan format for the absolute first time in your association, it's normal to not be right in a portion of your suppositions—particularly around objectives and gauging. In any case, what's significant, is that you cautiously report what necessities are refreshing when it's the ideal opportunity for a variant two of your business plan.

Characterize clear cutoff times and achievements in your business plan

So as to know whether the suspicions you're making in your business plan are near the imprint, you have to separate that large number into more modest desires with exacting cutoff times. We call these achievements, and they're amazingly convenient in following whether your business plan is in the correct way.

Clear cutoff times and sensible achievements set aside examination and effort to create. They should challenge and spur your business group without being so troublesome they murder spirit.

Once more, start with a year ago numbers (on the off chance that you have them). Track how to deal's incomes expanded every year and contrast your organization with the business guidelines. Converse with your business group about what they do during the weeks' worth of work, regardless of whether that is jumping on deals calls, prospecting new clients, or shutting bargains. Ask the amount they're at present doing and how much transmission capacity they need to accomplish more. This will give you a genuine, bleeding-edge take of what achievements to set in your business plan layout.

Next, it's an ideal opportunity to set your achievements. These should be explicit with clear objectives and cutoff times. For instance, you should build your client base by 20%

or increment deals half for a particular item. Or then again even increment the level of clients on a paid arrangement by 15% by mid-year. Whatever the achievement is, be clear what your desires are and set a hard cutoff time for your group to pursue.

Finally, set individual achievements for your business group also. These individual objectives need to consider the distinctions among your sales reps. On the off chance that somebody in your group is settling on a great deal of decisions, however not shutting, give them an achievement of increasing their nearby rate. In the event that somebody's extraordinary at shutting, however, doesn't make a lot of effort, give them an achievement of reaching ten new possibilities a month.

United, these achievements advise and uphold your general deals plan, giving you an unmistakable, noteworthy arrangement of how you will hit your general objectives for the year.

Pick a specialty to zero in on and assemble footing in

Since we recognize what we need to hit, how about we get into the bare essential of working out our business plan layout.

To begin with, we have to realize the market we're in and the specialty we will possess so we can appropriately situate our business for development (and to accomplish the objectives in your business plan).

What's a business specialty? Basically, it's what your business spends significant time in, yet it goes somewhat more profound than that. A specialty is a space your business involves, with your items; however, with your substance, your organization culture, your marking, and your message. It's the means by which individuals relate to you and search you out over the opposition.

"At the point when you attempt to make something for everybody, you wind up making something for nobody."

Rather, start by taking a gander at a specialty and asking yourself these inquiries:

- How large is the market?
- Is there an underlying interest in what you're selling?
- What's your present market position: Including any qualities, shortcomings, openings, or dangers
- Who are your rivals? What are their qualities, shortcoming, openings, and dangers?

In case you're trapped, start by returning to your own qualities — Rundown out your most grounded interests and interests. Pick a field where the chances are now in support of yourself, where you have a demonstrated history, more skill to offer, a broad contact base, and individuals who can give you introductions.

The magnificence of working in a field that you, as of now, have an enthusiasm for is that you can construct a foothold through turning into an idea chief. These sorts of vital favorable circumstances will enhance the outcomes you're ready to get from your business plan.

Do you have something special to state about your market? Blog, compose, and add to applicable distributions. Be a visitor on digital broadcasts. Talk at functions. Increase the value of the lives of your possibilities before you actually request that they become a client.

The greater permeability you can have in your specialty, the more possibility you have of hitting the objectives and achievements in your business plan.

Also, regardless of whether you center around one specialty, it doesn't mean your business can't develop. Start with one item in one specialty and afterward branch out to an integral specialty. Sell wonderful, handmade teacups? What about a flourishing doily business? Or then again adaptable teaspoons?

Comprehend your Objective Clients

It makes no sense investing energy and cash pursuing some unacceptable possibilities, so don't permit them to advance into your business plan.

When you know your specialty, it's an ideal opportunity to uncover into finding, however much as could be expected about your objective client so as to appropriately offer to them.

Anyway, exactly what would it be a good idea for you to hope to characterize your crowd inside your business plan? That relies upon your organization and your market, yet start with essentials like organization size (regarding representatives or turnover), topographical data, industry, work title, and so forth — any attributes that are basic over your best clients or the kinds of clients you'd love to have.

Additionally, remember to consider whether they will be a solid match'. On the off chance that this is a drawn-out relationship you're growing instead of a single night rendezvous, you need to ensure you're communicating in a similar language and offer a comparable culture and vision.

Utilize this data to work out an ideal client profile. This can be your ideal 'amazing client' or an invented association that gets a huge incentive from utilizing your item/administration, and furthermore gives noteworthy incentive to your organization.

A client profile causes you to qualify new leads and preclude ones preceding you go through months looking in the wrong place and under-conveying on your business plan.

When you know the sort of organization you need to focus on, it's an ideal opportunity to get inside their head. Start by hanging out where they hang out:

- Are they via online media? What's their organization of decision?
- Are they individuals from any Facebook or LinkedIn gatherings?
- Can you answer industry inquiries for them on Quora or Reddit?
- What web recordings do they tune in to, or what assets do they read?

Get in your clients' heads, and you'll be in a vastly improved situation to offer to them.

Guide out your client's excursion

Okay, presently, we're getting someplace strong.

With your optimal client profile set up, the following aspect of your business plan needs to address how that client turns into your client. We can do this by delineating their excursion from prospect to faithful client.

Anyway, what do we have to think about our prospective clients? We should begin with the fundamentals to ask them:

- What do you need our item to accomplish for you?
- What are the highlights imperative to you? Why?
- What's your financial plan for this?
- How would you say you are right now taking care of this issue?

These are, on the whole, incredible inquiries to pose Nonetheless, it's a gigantic slip-up to just zero in on the present in your business plan.

Incredible sales reps take their purchasers on an excursion through time — from before they even realized they required your answer for when they're an upbeat, steadfast client. To completely comprehend their excursion as a client, start by getting some information about past purchasing encounters:

- When was the last time you purchased something like our administration or item?
- Was that a fortunate or unfortunate experience? Why?
- How did you settle on your choice in those days? How was the dynamic cycle?
- How did you assess various offers?
- What were the main factors that made you picked that specific arrangement?

THE OPENING SALES

On the off chance that they had an incredible past encounter, consider approaches to adjust your pitch to that insight and separate yourself with your extraordinary offer (more on this next!). In the event that they had a terrible encounter, separation yourself, and clarify how you would fix that circumstance.

Next, get your possibility to characterize their own guide to a near to asking them, 'what's straightaway?'

In the event that the state, they'll need to get the endorsement from the VP of Finance. Inquire:

"Alright, and suppose he concurs that we're the correct fit, what's straightaway?"

Placing your possibility in this future-considering state of mind causes them to envision purchasing from you. This is an amazing asset, which can help reveal any expected barricades and even assistance quicken the business cycle.

In your business plan layout, make certain to address the whole client venture from pre-to post-deal.

Characterize your incentives

We know our clients. We know their excursion. Presently we have to fit ourselves into it in an ideal manner conceivable. This originates from characterizing your upper hand.

Your upper hand is the thing that separates you from the opposition, which completely understanding and articulating is an urgent component of your business plan format. Start by posing a couple of straightforward inquiries:

- Why do clients purchase from us?
- Why do clients purchase from our rivals and not us?
- Why do some potential clients not accepting by any stretch of the imagination?
- What do we have to do to be fruitful later on?

Recall that clients purchase benefits, not highlights. While portraying your offer, it's anything but difficult to become involved with discussing you. What you've made. What you do. Rather, turn the tables and discussion about what your item will accomplish for your clients. A solid upper hand:

- Reflects the serious quality of your business
- Is ideally, yet not really, extraordinary
- Is clear and straightforward
- May change after some time as contenders attempt to take your thought
- Must be upheld by continuous statistical surveying

THE OPENING SALES

It isn't so much that your helpdesk programming has online media reconciliations and constant ticket following that is important to most clients. The reality makes their carries on with simpler and permits them to zero in on what they care about most: Creating an extraordinary client experience instead of monitoring what that one client said on Twitter a week ago.

Zero in on esteem, not highlights in your business plan layout

Your upper hand isn't only a fundamental aspect of your business plan, yet you will advise everything your organization does pushing ahead, from advertising to item improvement.

It's an incredible case of where deals can impact the improvement of an item and the course of business.

Manufacture a possibility list

Since you know the sorts of clients you're after and how you will sell them, it's an ideal opportunity to work out the elite of individuals at these organizations to start deals prospecting. A possibility list is a place we take all the hypotheses and examination of the last hardly any segments of our business plan layout and put them energetically.

At its center, a possibility list is an index of genuine individuals you can contact who might profit from your item or administration. This can be a tedious undertaking; however, it's fundamental for driving your business plan and friends' development.

To begin with, utilize your optimal client profile to begin discovering objective organizations:

- Search LinkedIn
- Check out applicable neighborhood business organizations
- Attend organizing functions and meetups
- Do basic Google look
- Check out the part rundown of pertinent online gatherings

Focus up to 5 individuals at every association (you can generally move horizontally towards the correct purchaser regardless of who in the association really reacts to you). Focusing on more than one individual will give you better chances for associating on a cool effort just as a superior possibility that somebody in your organization can interface you actually.

Keep in mind; this isn't only a huge rundown of individuals you could offer to.

THE OPENING SALES

This is focused on a list dependent on the exploration you've done beforehand in your business plan. One might say, a strong deals plan format qualifies your possibilities before you even go through brief conversing with them.

When you have your rundown, monitor your leads and how you discovered them utilizing a business CRM. This will keep the verifiable setting incivility and ensure you don't cover on outreach in case you're working with partners.

Influence current customer connections

"At last, practically all product organizations wind up getting ~80% or so of their new clients from their current clients once they hit scale. From references. From brand. From informal." –

SaaStr originator Jason Lemkin

You're passing up an immense chance if your business plan format just spotlights on finding new business leads. Informal presentations and current clients can be your most strong lead for development.

Use LinkedIn to check whether anybody you know can acquaint you with one of your possibilities. Or then again, connect with your most faithful clients and inquire as to whether they know anybody that would profit by your item or administration (you can significantly offer a reference reward or limited rate).

Presently, when utilizing current customer connections in your business plan, you'll have to ensure you do it in the correct manner. When requesting an introduction, recollect:

- A great presentation is two-sided: As the individual in the center, you're approaching your customer to vouch for you. In the event that you, as of now, have a decent relationship, this ought to be an easy decision. You offered some benefit to them, and they should need to help you thusly. Ask them how well they know your objective. Would they feel great acquainting you with them? By telephone? Over email? A decent presentation shouldn't emerge from the blue. Request that they ensure it's OK to the introduction and afterward cc you in on an email with the two players.
- Stay in contact, in any event, when they can't accepting from you: Ask how you can help or support them, regardless of whether they quit being a client. It's a little signal that can pay off over the long haul. Things don't remain the equivalent for long.

Recognize vital accomplices (that arrive at similar clients)

THE OPENING SALES

The last gathering you ought to remember for your business plan layout are any key accomplices—people, associations, or organizations—that arrive at similar clients. A few people call these Complementary Service Providers (CSPs) as they aren't the opposition and rather offer some item or administration that supplements yours.

For instance, in case you're selling a POS framework for nearby stores, you could contact a retail association like the California Retailers Association or a regarded neighborhood business specialist.

Plan to construct your relationship with these gatherings through things like:

- They are writing for their distribution.
- Giving talks at workshops
- Providing assets for their sites
- Starting a brains bunch where you can trade contacts

Keep in mind; you ought to offer these administrations for nothing out of pocket and fuse that time interest in your business plan format.

It's tied in with offering some incentive to correlative organizations and cultivating a culture of 'becoming together.' The more you enhance the network, the more individuals will need to send drives your direction.

You're not done at this point! Track, measure, and change varying

Because you've made a strong deals plan layout to follow doesn't mean you get the opportunity to kick back and watch the money move in. Recollect what Basecamp organizer Jason Fried said about plans:

"An arrangement is basically a theory you recorded."

You're utilizing all that you think about the market, your special worth, target clients, and accomplices to characterize the ideal circumstance for your organization. Be that as it may, truly, attempt as we may, not many of us really observe anything when we look profound into the precious stone ball.

Rather, recollect that your business plan is an absolutely real doc and simply, like the remainder of your organization, needs to represent and adjust to new highlights, advertising efforts, or even new colleagues who join. You have to re-visitation of it routinely to evaluate whether your suppositions are transforming into the real world.

Set customary gatherings (at any rate month to month) to audit progress on your business plan, distinguish and comprehend issues, and adjust your exercises across groups to enhance your arrangement around genuine functions and input. Gain from your errors and triumphs, and develop your business plan varying.

THE OPENING SALES

In many deal circumstances, the greatest test is idleness. However, with a strong, point by point deals plan and a devoted group with clear achievements set up, you'll have all you require to push through any measure of erosion and keep on target to hit your objectives!

THE OPENING SALES

Chapter 2: Sales Algorithm

Actualizing business cycles can smooth out the consummation of any errand, basic or complex. Cycles can likewise make your representatives more productive, steady, and exact both in their jobs and their collaborations with clients.

The advantages of cycles in business apply to your business division also. A business cycle that supplements your business, agents, clients, and items or administrations will permit you to help changes, close more arrangements, and guarantee the entirety of your reps are furnishing clients with positive and reliable encounters — regardless of who they're conversing with.

Nonetheless, building an adaptable and repeatable deals cycle can be intense, particularly in light of the fact that each business, deals group, and target crowd is novel.

We've made this manual to help you. Underneath, you'll locate the best strategies to make and guide a business cycle custom-made to your business that works for both your business group and target crowd.

2.1 Sales Process

A business cycle alludes to a repeatable arrangement of stages a business group takes to move a possibility from a beginning phase lead to a shut client. A solid deals measure helps reps reliably close arrangements by giving them a system to follow.

Before we spread the subtleties of making and planning your business cycle, how about we audit the response to a typical inquiry: What's the distinction between a business cycle and a business system?

Sales Process versus Deals Methodology

Understanding the qualification between a business cycle and deals approach is significant. Albeit firmly related, a business cycle and deals strategy are two altogether different things.

As we inspected above, a business cycle is a solid arrangement of activities your business group follows to close another client.

A business system is a structure for how your business cycle is to be completed and how it will enable your business to develop.

Here's an outline to assist you with envisioning this:

Think about your business cycle as the elevated level guide of the means your group takes, while your business procedures are the various ways your group can move toward the business cycle.

Sales Methodologies

Picking a business strategy sets the establishment for your group as they approach your business cycle. You may decide to join one as they are another approach to smooth out your client's purchaser travel and guarantee proficient, significant, and supportive connections between those clients and your business group happen.

Here are five mainstream deals strategies.

Challenger Sales Methodology

The Challenger Sales technique is a way to deal with deals that says the dealer, or Challenger, must show the possibility. Venders find out about a client's business, tailor their offering procedures to their requirements and trouble spots, and challenge any of their assumptions all through the cycle.

Arrangement Selling

Arrangement selling expects reps to zero in exclusively on the client's trouble spots rather than the items or administrations they're selling. Items are outlined as arrangements, and accentuation is set on what a goal for the client's pinpoint.

Sandler Sales Methodology

The Sandler Sales approach says the purchaser and merchant have similarly put resources into the business cycle. Reps are prepared to address client complaints early, so significant time is put aside for the two players. The purchaser is practically persuading the merchant to make the deal.

Consultative Selling

Consultative selling places accentuation on the sales rep turning into a confided in guide to the client, picking up power and trust after some time. Consultative selling happens when deals line up with the client's purchasing experience — the client rep relationship characterizes it.

Inbound Selling

The inbound deals approach is portrayed by pulling in purchasers with customized and pertinent substance instead of promoting immaterial messages and trusting they'll purchase.

THE OPENING SALES

Source

With endless decisions in the present commercial center, it's significant for deals groups to put their purchasers' necessities in front of their own.

The inbound methodology originated from the conviction that:

- Buyers would now be able to discover most of the data (on the web or elsewhere) they need about an organization's items or administrations before they draw in with a sales rep.
- Buyers have gotten better at shutting unconscious and interruptive deals procedures (cold pitches and unimportant deals messages, for instance).
- Buyers have uplifted desires around the experience of purchasing. They can control the experience and travel through the cycle generally on their own course of events.

These movements in purchasing patterns are largely instances of how purchasers have held onto control of the business cycle from the salesmen who once held all the force.

In view of these changes, it's significant for deals groups to receive a more supportive, human way to deal with selling — or inbound selling.

2.2 Sales Process Steps

1. Prospect.
2. Connect and qualify.
3. Research.
4. Present.
5. Handle complaints.
6. Close.
7. Communicate and keep on selling.

Since we've secured the contrast between a business cycle and strategy, we should audit the six stages of the business cycle so you can start creating one for your group.

Prospect

Prospecting is the way toward sourcing new, beginning phase prompts to start working through the business cycle. It's a crucial aspect of the business cycle and part of most reps' every day or week by the week work process.

Prospecting may include online examination on locales like LinkedIn or Quora. It additionally may occur at gatherings or industry functions. Moreover, you can prospect by asking current customers or associates to allude people who may be keen on your item or administration.

Interface and qualify

The interface step of the business cycle includes reps starting contact with those beginning phase prompts accumulate data. The second aspect of this progression qualifying new leads — choosing whether or not they're a solid match lead for your business and whether they'll probably push ahead in the purchaser's excursion.

A rep can normally decide this over an "interface" or "revelation" call (once in a while over email if not through telephone). To do this, a rep may pose qualifying inquiries like:

- "What is your part inside your organization?"
- "What do you do every day?"
- "What issue would you say you are attempting to illuminate?"
- "Why is this a need for your business?"
- "What different arrangements would you say you are assessing?"

Exploration

Next comes the exploration step, when reps become familiar with each prospect and friends. This permits your reps to offer a more custom-made and customized insight and improves the probability of finalizing a negotiation.

This stage's key aspect is seeing each prospect's difficulties and needs and building up how your item or administration can help.

This may require a rep to talk with others at the organization in various offices to get an all-encompassing perspective on the business and its targets. Numerous long-term reps state a decent salesman comprehends the organization in a better way than the individual possibility that works there.

Present

The introduction step is regularly when your salesman runs a proper introduction or showing off your item or administration for your possibility.

This progression is tedious, so it regularly comes further in the business cycle and is saved for more genuine possibilities — which is the reason the associating and qualifying step is so basic. You don't need your reps burning through any of their significant time if it's obviously avoidable.

THE OPENING SALES

Every introduction ought to be custom-made to meet the particular possibility's extraordinary use case and trouble spots. Also, a rep may carry a specialist or leader to the gathering with them to show the degree of administration the client will get while working with your organization. This likewise permits them to respond to more specialized inquiries the rep probably won't be most appropriate to remark on.

Handle protests

It's normal for possibilities to have issues with your salesman's introduction and proposition. Truth be told, it's normal — which is the reason this is a particular advance in the business cycle. Your business group ought to be set up to deal with any complaints. Tuning in to your possibility's protests and questions can enable your reps to all the more likely tailor your item to meet their requirements.

Through their examination and introduction arrangement, reps ought to recognize and foresee potential protests, regardless of whether relating to cost, onboarding, or different pieces of the proposed agreement.

Close

This progression of the business cycle alludes to any late-organize exercises that occur as an arrangement approaches shutting. It changes broadly from organization to organization and may incorporate things like conveying a statement or proposition, exchange, or accomplishing the upfront investment of chiefs.

The nearby advance is the thing that each salesman runs after. It should bring about a commonly gainful, legally binding understanding between the possibility and the dealer. When an arrangement shuts, the sales rep gets a commission on the value they haggled with the client, and the record ordinarily passes to a record administrator or client achievement agent.

Convey and keep on selling

Albeit shutting bargains is a definitive objective in deals, it's not where salespeople quit working with clients. In addition to the fact that reps should direct that clients get what they've bought, they should likewise impact changing clients to whichever group is answerable for onboarding and client achievement.

The last advance of the business cycle likewise includes proceeding to convey and fortify an incentive to clients. This can give occasions to upsell and strategically pitch to clients just as secure references from pleased clients.

Next, we should unload how you can improve this cycle.

2.3 The most effective method to Improve Your Sales Process

1. Analyze your present sales measure.
2. Layout the purchaser's excursion for your objective persona.
3. Define the possibility of activity that moves them to the following stage.
4. Define leave standards for each progression of the sales cycle.
5. Measure your sales cycle results.

These four prescribed procedures will help you improve the effectiveness of your sales cycle over your group and client base.

Examine your present sales measure

Consider what is and isn't working for both your sales reps and the possibilities to tailor your new cycle to more readily meet their requirements. This will help close more arrangements and enjoyment for more clients.

One approach to dissect your present sales measure's achievement is to watch reps as they work through the sales cycle.

Glance back at the last five or 10 gives you shut. What did these arrangements resemble from start to finish? What was the touch focuses on the client?

Consider generally what amount of time the whole cycle required and how long slipped by between each progression. The more models you have (and the more individuals in your group those models originate from), the better.

Whenever you've recognized that course of events, work in reverse to comprehend the timetable for each arrangement. For instance, if six of those ten arrangements shut in around a month and a half, investigate what the normal advances were to arrive during that time-frame.

Working in reverse may look something like this:

- One seven day stretch of consideration before a marked agreement (during the "end" step)
- Three-to-five subsequent messages and calls (during the "dealing with complaints" step)
- One demo (during the "introducing" step)
- One call and a few messages (during the "investigating" step)
- One disclosure call (during the "interfacing" step)
- Two warm messages and three calls to prospect (during the "prospecting" step)

THE OPENING SALES

You can likewise burrow somewhat more profound to comprehend the unobtrusive inspirations and trouble spots that drove each arrangement to close.

Spread out the purchaser's excursion for your objective persona

Spread out the purchaser's excursion for your intended interest group or your purchaser personas. This will permit you to take a gander at your sales cycle from the viewpoint of your clients. You'll have the option to improve comprehension of the cooperations they have with your reps, the problem areas they experience, and why they need your item or administration.

At the point when you spread out the purchaser's excursion for your objective persona, you'll pick up knowledge into how you can tailor your sales cycle to guarantee your group has all they require to assemble solid associations with possibilities and close more arrangements.

Characterize the possibility activity that moves them to the following stage

Get away from what makes a possible move starting with one phase then onto the next to truly comprehend your sales cycle. In a perfect world, the explanation or cause will be founded on the possibility's activities, not the view of the sales rep.

To decide the activity that moves possibilities to the following stage, pose the accompanying inquiries:

- "While leading warm effort, did a rep hit on a particular agony point(s) that persuaded the possibility to plan a disclosure call?"
- "During the demo, were there protests that slowed down the arrangement or included that pushed it ahead?"
- When a rep made a pitch, was the appropriate response a prompt "yes" from the client? Assuming this is the case, consider cautiously why that occurred. How could they develop to the pitch?

Characterize leave measures for each progression of the sales cycle

Characterize leave rules for each progression of the sales cycle for your group. This implies you ought to distinguish the things that need to occur for your possibilities to move from one stage of your sales cycle to the following. You can allude to the sales cycle steps and the means of the purchaser's excursion (as referenced above) to begin with this.

For instance, in case you're working through the "introducing" step, your reps may decide they need a particular sort of substance —, for example, client tribute recordings — to impart to your possibilities to move them to "shutting."

When deciding way out rules for each progression of the sales cycle, consider the accompanying inquiries to guarantee the entirety of your reps have similar data so they can furnish the entirety of your possibilities with positive, proficient, and on-brand data.

- What data should reps think about your image, whatever it is they're selling, and your sales cycle ventures before getting in contact with a possibility?
- What moves should your reps make all through each progression of the sales cycle?
- What should your reps state all through each progression of the sales cycle? Ensure your reps know about the different ways a discussion might go and that they realize how to deal with every one of them.
- What explicit sorts of substance should your reps show your possibilities during various strides of the sales cycle? This is particularly significant in the "introducing" step, where your reps may need to furnish your possibilities with recordings, websites, tributes, or contextual analyses to move that prospect to close.

Measure your sales cycle results

It's reasonable your sales cycle will advance as your group discovers approaches to work all the more productively and move possibilities through your pipeline quicker. As you characterize and improve your sales cycle after some time, you'll need to quantify your prosperity to guarantee your sales cycle is effective in organizing the endeavors of your group and arriving at your intended interest group.

For instance, take a gander at the number of possibilities changed into and out of each progression of the sales cycle in a given time span.

This way, you can make determinations like, "In July, we began with 75 possibilities in the 'anticipating demo' step ... toward the month's end, we had traveled through 28 possibilities, and included 19, leaving us with 66 possibilities in the 'anticipating demo' step."

Here are some different instances of measurements to consider for the various strides of your cycle:

- The normal time possibilities remain in each progression.

THE OPENING SALES

- The step (assuming any) that takes excessively long for possibilities to move out of
- The level of possibilities who close after a demo
- The level of possibilities who demand a demo after a disclosure call
- The agitate rate (i.e., if certain clients are beating rapidly, how might you utilize this information to recognize confounded possibilities from the get-go in the sales cycle?)

These are the fundamental measurements most groups discover an incentive in estimating. Think about measurements explicit to your business that will assist you with characterizing achievement or the requirement for development in a specific advance.

Figure out how to make a vigorous, purchaser driven sales measure with our free HubSpot Academy exercise How to Map a Sales Process.

Another extraordinary method to gauge your outcomes is with the three degrees of sales measure achievement. Figuring out which level of progress you're in will give you more understanding of what it is you have to adjust for your group and prospects as far as your sales cycle.

Humming

Your sales cycle is murmuring when 80% or a greater amount of your reps are hitting their standard consistently. This is additionally when the entirety of your recently recruited employees are being inclined up rapidly to target execution, and your group isn't giving you any negative input about the sales cycle.

Experimenting

Testing is the point at which your sales cycle isn't exactly murmuring, so your group is testing and testing various strategies inside the means of the sales cycle to figure out what's best for reps.

For instance, a group may be exploring different avenues regarding various methods of contact in the "interfacing" step of the sales cycle to get sales conversations moving with possibilities. They can test to see whether their possibilities react best to a particular email format while kicking a conversation off with a rep.

Thrashing

Whipping is the point at which a group is quickly moving, starting with one arrangement then onto the next inside a particular advance of the sales cycle. Whipping is insufficient, and something you'll need to guarantee your group escapes as fast as could be expected under the circumstances in case you're regularly encountering it.

For instance, your reps may be attempting diverse introduction methods in the "introducing" stage, making it difficult to truly figure out what's working for most of the possibilities.

Keep in mind; your sales cycle is rarely awesome. It ought to consistently be advancing to fit the requirements of your group, business, and possibilities.

2.4 Model on How to Map the Sales Process

Planning your sales cycle is the act of strolling through each progression continuously and seeing how it applies to your business, sales group, and clients.

This cycle permits you to reveal shortcomings, gain knowledge into what's working, and adjust your sales cycle with your business objectives. It enables your group to build up a feasible methodology appropriate for long haul development.

At the point when you map your sales cycle, you answer the "why" behind each choice you make — which is basic in light of the fact that your sales cycle is the establishment of everything your group does. How about we stroll through how to plan the sales cycle utilizing an anecdotal business model.

Start toward the end

To realize where you're going, you should know your objective. Regarding sales measure planning, this includes defining objectives for your sales group. Keep your objective explicit yet straightforward.

Model:

Fred's Vegan Food Supply is planning their sales cycle. They've set their "objective" to build their success rate by 5% next quarter.

Bring all partners on board

Your sales group can't meet its objective alone. Different divisions over your association — including showcasing, item, client care, IT, and that's just the beginning — have a stake in your sales cycle and affect your client experience. Assemble these partners, share your objective, and include them in your cycle.

Model:

Fred unites his sales group, showcasing directors, client assistance pioneers, item fashioners, and wholesalers. These groups contact potential and current clients and can, in this way, influence the sales group's success rate.

THE OPENING SALES

Guide the sales cycle steps

We secured the sales cycle ventures above, and now it's an ideal opportunity to stroll through each progression in accordance with your business, items, and sales group. Investigate your sales cycle history. What steps were viable, and where did possibilities tumble off? Overall, did each progression take? Likewise, with your partners ready, you can plan what groups influence each progression and what moves they can make — especially your sales group.

Model:

Fred's sales group maps the six sales measure steps and scribbles down the moves they make inside each stage. They additionally audit the most recent a year of sales action as for each progression to all the more likely comprehend where they can improve their new sales cycle to meet their new objective.

Guide the purchaser's excursion

Next, investigate your sales cycle from the client's viewpoint. On a similar record, write down your clients' activities and responses to your sales cycle. Keep your purchaser personas convenient while doing this to guarantee your group stays client-driven.

Model:

Fred's sales group currently maps the purchaser's excursion inside their set up sales measure. By adjusting these activities, the group can recognize where their group is encountering shortcomings, what steps are functioning admirably, and where they have to improve to meet their objective.

Execute changes, test, and measure

Whenever you've planned your sales cycle from both the merchant's and purchaser's points of view, you're prepared to give it something to do. You won't know whether the cycle will help with your objective until you test it and measure the outcomes.

Model:

Fred puts his new sales measure in real life with his group. They stroll through each stage and the suitable activities, and they give close consideration to how their client's demonstration and respond. As they travel through each stage and towards their new objective, they change the pieces of their cycle that aren't working so easily.

2.5 Sales Process Common Mistakes

We should investigate some basic missteps made when creating sales measures. These will assist you in building up a sales cycle ideal for both your group and clients.

Leaving your sales cycle steps not entirely clear

It's critical to characterize explicit, solid activities that move your business' possibilities starting with one phase then onto the next. In the event that you don't distinguish these triggers, your sales group may leave away with a not exactly precise comprehension of what is and isn't working for possibilities, conceivably making them misuse part of the cycle.

When you characterize your sales cycle, record it, share it, and practice it with your group. Attempt pretend activities to commute home the significant methods they ought to be making during each stride.

Anticipating only one sales philosophy (in the event that you utilize one) to be the "silver slug."

While a few groups decide to stay with and follow one technique intently, others decide to contemplate a few famous sales procedures and consolidate pieces and pieces they find valuable from each.

Notwithstanding which approach you take, it's a smart thought to remain mindful of what's happening and changing after some time. As the requirements and wants of purchasers and your business change, various methodologies, strategies, and methods of dealing with your sales cycle will become into and undesirable.

On that note, it's imperative to recall your whole sales measure is additionally ever-evolving.

Overlooking your sales cycle will consistently be a work in progress

Your sales cycle is rarely finished or awesome. It ought to consistently be a work in progress. Along these lines, notwithstanding reliably estimating your prosperity, you ought to likewise have registration with your reps, who are working through your sales cycle each day and speaking with possibilities, consistently to guarantee they haven't revealed any significant issues or warnings concerning your cycle.

Keep in mind, consistently creating and improving your sales cycle will make crafted by your reps more direct and improve the associations and encounters your clients have with your reps and business overall.

Plunge Into Your Sales Process

THE OPENING SALES

Making and planning a sales cycle will enable your sales to group close more arrangements and convert more leads. This will likewise guarantee your group furnishes each prospect with a similar kind of steady insight, delegate of your image.

Follow these means to make and guide a sales cycle customized to your business, sales group, and clients to start boosting changes and building enduring connections today.

2.6 Common Sense Matters a Lot

Most organizations spend them promoting financial plans producing market mindfulness and sales leads; however, they spend valuable small outfitting their sales power with the information and instruments to sell. What's more, in the present questionable economy, selling is definitely not simple.

That is the reason for building up a powerful sales guide or introduction for your group is so basic. It doesn't make a difference, whether it's a printed manage or a computerized rendition. A decent sales control instructs your sales power on the best way to position and offer your contributions to the possibilities well on the way to purchase.

So let's investigate a straightforward, bit by bit measure that will promise you to produce a successful and famous offering archive to amplify your group's sales changes.

A compelling Sales Guide capacities as a source of the perspective instrument, sorting out subtleties for snappy admittance to assist sales with peopling assume responsibility for the sales cycle.

It assists with building trust in your contribution, so sales individuals feel good introducing it to clients, managing protests, and defying the opposition.

Furthermore, a decent sales direct rouses your sales power to sell.

Lamentably, numerous organizations distribute insufficient sales manages that can, at last, reason income to slip. In any case, it doesn't need to be that way. Follow these six key advances and prepare for a change in your sales picture.

Stage 1: Make sure you include the sales power

Numerous organizations create sales guides with practically zero contributions from the individuals who really use them—the sales power. The outcome is a printed or advanced archive that is detached from their true difficulties and just serves to extend the gorge among sales and advertising.

THE OPENING SALES

To build up viable sales control, it's fundamental that you converse with the sales group and get them to "purchase in" to the entire thought of a methodical way to deal with their introductions. All things considered, it's to their greatest advantage with regards to acquiring higher commissions!

So pick their cerebrums to realize what they generally consider helpful — and generally disappointing — in sales guides, they've utilized previously.

Stage 2: Provide an outline of exceptional serious data

Sales direct frequently paint a too-blushing perspective on the organization's serious position or contain serious obsolete data. Take a gander at it from the sales group's point of view — how might you want to do battle with wrong information on your adversary's qualities, shortcomings, and position comparative with your own? It resembles attempting to win a blade battle with your best arm tied behind your back!

So give the sales power what they have to win. Get an outsider to contact your three primary rivals and solicitation their writing. Investigate their sites. Check whether you can acquire their value records. At that point, give a fair-minded synopsis of their qualities and shortcomings, and clarify with definite content aides how to deal with your own item or administration weaknesses when conversing with possibilities.

Situating your item against a contender's shortcomings is simple — it's the rival's qualities that represent a test.

Stage 3: Motivate the opening of new records and income streams

Sales individuals feel gigantic strain to create. Their positions are consistently on the line, so they normally search out the quickest, surest course to accomplishing their objectives.

Be that as it may, the quickest course might be what's recognizable — the current product offering or client base — instead of what's going on. Your test is to inspire the sales power to offer to new chances.

A compelling sales manager must "sell" sales individuals on new items or applications before you can anticipate that they should offer to other people. So incorporate client examples of overcoming adversity, contextual analyses, and tributes that help construct the contribution's validity to the sales rep, just as clients.

Stage 4: Respect the sales power's time

Sales individuals are continually barraged with data about items, changes, updates, exceptional offers, and so forth. The exact opposite thing they need is a protracted, scattered Powerpoint, PDF, or printed record that neglects to assist them with finding significant data when they need it.

So endeavor to build up a succinct, simple to-utilize sales control. Be finicky about the data you incorporate. Sort out your substance by contemplating the regular progression of inquiries a sales individual would pose to another possibility.

Make it simple for sales individuals to rapidly discover what they need. Use outlines and tables at whatever point conceivable to gather a lot of data, and guarantee that your sales manager is intriguing to peruse.

Stage 5: Make the recommendation of the sales UNIQUE and SPECIFIC

Be careful with nonexclusive messages or destroyed expressions that no one takes any notification of. This is the fastest method to ensure the contrasts between your contributions and those of your rivals are lost on your clients.

Sales individuals need a CONCISE PRODUCT DEFINITION, a UNIQUE VALUE PROPOSITION, and a SUCCINCT SALES SCRIPT or guide. Without this, you will be winning just a little division of all the business you could without much of a stretch be catching.

Stage 6: Choose your author cautiously

Sales individuals frequently grumble that sales aides or introductions contain too little data to be valuable or a lot of specialized detail to try perusing. So for what reason do countless sales guides miss the mark concerning the imprint and end up left on the rack or unopened on the PC?

The inclinations and foundation of the sales control journalists are typically the guilty parties. At the point when composed by promoting staff, sales aides may avoid specialized detail. At the point when composed by specialized staff, selling data might be overlooked. Neither one of the groups may comprehend the sales cycle.

Also, the specific composition and wide business abilities that sales guides require are not normally an occupation necessity for sales, promoting, or specialized faculty.

Great sales manage essayists can make an interpretation of specialized data into straightforward, available language; however, they're acquainted with the sales cycle and have advertising bowed.

THE OPENING SALES

What's more, they're talented in rapidly recognizing the most significant components in monstrous measures of data and combining them into a tight, clear composition.

On the off chance that none of your workers have this blend of abilities, or if the ideal competitor doesn't have the ability to finish the venture rapidly, you might need to consider employing an accomplished sales introduction/direct designer.

2.7 Keep Moving Forward

You distinguished the ideal customer for your administration. You made a heavenly introduction with explicit instances of how your organization is able to address the customer's needs. You rehearsed your pitch, and you're sure. You nailed the introduction.

Also, after the entirety of that, they said, "no." You're squashed. You're left scrutinizing your vocation decision and your capacities.

In case you're in a sales position, and it hasn't transpired at this point, it will. What do you do now?

Before you discount that forthcoming customer, you actually have some basic work to do. It's anything but difficult to harp on the negative insight and leave; however, you might be leaving a future arrangement on the table. What's more, you may pick up something fundamental in case you're sufficiently striking to ask some subsequent inquiries.

Here are five different ways to remain positive and to push ahead regardless of a dismissal:

Request input

It's difficult to do, yet it won't hurt. Inquire as to why they settled on the choice to go with another firm or to leave the arrangement.

At the point when you request helpful analysis, you may be shocked by what you hear, and you may get more knowledge into how they settled on the choice.

Think about the analysis and practice situations that utilize the recommendations. Utilize their reactions to roll out future improvements. Perhaps you'll understand this possibility wasn't an astounding possibility regardless. Each dismissal can assist you with bettering build up who your optimal customer is, and from that point, the ideal approach to finalize the negotiation.

THE OPENING SALES

Tolerating productive analysis with a receptive outlook takes practice. Listen cautiously (and unobtrusively!) and take notes. Thank the possibility consciously.

Follow up

Subsequent meet-ups are important for the game. All things considered, it takes five contact endeavors to get a "yes." That doesn't mean you should barrage your place of contact. Check-in occasionally so you're at the forefront of their thoughts.

There are numerous reasons individuals state no, and it's possible the appropriate response isn't close to home. Possibly your administration or prospect won't be affirmed in the current year's spending plan. Begin preparing: build up when their spending year starts, and all the more critically when they submit spending things so you can connect heretofore with a refreshed proposition.

Get a feeling of what they need to find in a proposition. Here and there, it pays to be wide, while on different occasions, it's ideal to be more explicit. Maybe they weren't prepared for your wide proposition, and you can introduce a pared-down form sometime in the future.

Keep in mind; it's OK, to begin with, a more modest purchase since you can include administrations and things as you gain trust. Those 98 percent who said "no" on the main gathering esteem trust almost as much as they esteem the administration you give. Fabricate that relationship, and you will be at the forefront of their thoughts when they have a requirement for what you offer.

Stay in contact expertly

Show your reach; you esteem them as an expert association and thought pioneer in their industry. These are a couple of basic things you can do to give you give it a second thought:

- Connect on LinkedIn: This is a basic method to show you're keen on their profession. A straightforward "like" or remark can go far.
- Ask on the off chance that they'd prefer to be added to your mailing list: This is an extraordinary method to stay up with the latest on the news and show you're considering them when you convey occasion cards.
- Send an article: Read an article about a comparable effective business in another market? Send it alongside a speedy email and notice you thought they'd think that it's quick.

At the point when a purchaser feels an association, they are 60% bound to pay for your administrations. These endeavors help improve your organization's administrations and aptitudes, and your potential customer will become more acquainted with your business better from a far distance. You give them an opportunity to figure out how your administration or item bodes well for their business without the weight that goes with dynamic prospecting.

Request references

Maybe you're not actually some tea; however, perhaps their school flat mate who claims a business could utilize your administration. Reveal to them you trust in your administration or item, and you'd love the occasion to talk about it with somebody they think about a decent possibility. Direct correspondence can be scary; however, it will assist you with arriving at your objectives or draw near to them.

In case you're awkward with causing this to ask, offer a motivation for references—it'll make the signal appealing, and it's more probable your imminent customer will make sure to allude you.

Development with advertising materials your planned customer can ship off their partners in the event that they're requested a reference. Furthermore, remember to consistently incorporate contact data in your email signature, so you're anything but difficult to track down in their contacts.

You can even energize references inactively by offering individual outside references on your site, substantial reference cards, or systems administration through Facebook Groups or Meet up.

You've posed the inquiries and taken notes. What's straightaway?

Consider passing the possibility onto another rep

You're in sales, so you're serious, yet you probably won't be the correct character fit for this customer. Your supervisor needs the business, and you'll get a gesture of congratulations regardless of whether another person closes it.

Doing as such, the potential customer may see you as an important asset, and by presenting associations, you position yourself as somebody who is anything but difficult to work with and doesn't think about things too literally.

The whole group profits from new customers. Regardless of who made sure about it, a wide base of business broadens the organization's acknowledgment, and that will make more leads for all.

Converse with a confided in the guide and recollect it's OK. Have espresso with a coach or companion and request that they give you some legit criticism. You should, as of now, be doing this routinely, so this is the ideal occasion to look for guidance about your methodology.

Ask them what sales procedures work best in their industry. How would they continue hustling when they get a dismissal?

It's truly hard to hold your head up when you have portions to address and issue commissions to cover tabs. You gave a valiant effort, and they settled on a business choice that probably has nothing to do with you, actually. Utilize this as an occasion to reflect, roll out fundamental improvements, and develop.

THE OPENING SALES

Conclusion

The least demanding aspect of any sales call is the opening. It's the market aspect where there's no tension on you to make things work by any means. If someone says "no way" before you've even addressed him for five minutes – he'll have spared you a ton of time sometime later. Figuring out how to open a sales call is significant; however, you need to boost the odds that the individual on the opposite stopping point will need to hear more from you.

Opening a sales call is, in reality, extremely simple; it is a necessary cycle. Anybody can open a sales call, and, in the creator's insight, it's the piece of selling that a great many people appreciate. Why? — Because there's no genuine weight now in the call.

You don't have anything put resources into the relationship now; no statements have gone out; no costly leaflets have been sent, and the danger to your business at the kickoff of a sales call is nil.

Become familiar with The Basics of Opening a Sales Call

Welcome the Person

You'd be stunned at the number of telesales people, and even eye to eye salespeople overlook this and jump-start into talking out their pitch. Sales are genuinely about making connections, and connections are established upon social comforts and merriments. Welcome somebody isn't a discretionary extra – it's outright acceptable habits. Remember, like Will Rogers; the American entertainer said, "You will never get another opportunity to establish the first connection."

Keep your welcome formal except if you realize that the customer has a specific working method that precludes that. "Hello, Mrs. Singh" is superior to "Hi, Mrs. Peter," which is better than "Greetings, Mrs. Singh," which thus actually demolishes, "Yo! Mr. Peter! How's it going?"

Keep your welcome deferential and expert.

In up close and personal gatherings, we regularly start presenting ourselves with a handshake. That is impossible via telephone—so you need to introduce yourself verbally.

Present Yourself and Your Business

The stunt with this is to make yourself sound fascinating while at the same time guaranteeing that you don't give your customer any space to close the entryway in your face.

Best practice: "My name is XXX; I'm the CEO of XYZ Company. We're a nearby business that attempts to assist organizations with enjoying yours get more cash-flow."

Is there anyone out there who would not like to get more cash-flow? (Or on the other hand, if your administration is based around helping the client set aside cash, substitute "set aside cash" for "get more cash-flow.")

In the event that you state, "We're a nearby business that works in creating preparing for organizations like yours." They can say, "We as of now have a preparation supplier, much obliged." — And end the discussion.

To locate an unclear snare and utilize that instead of determining what you do. It's a lot simpler to proceed with a discussion where the advantage to a potential customer is clear than to proceed with one where the customer thinks, "Goodness, we as of now do that." — And turns off.

Express gratitude toward Them for Taking the Time

This virtually accepts that the individual will give you some time. Rather than requesting a space in their day (and everybody is occupied – in the event that you ask length, individuals will without a doubt reveal to you they are too occupied to even think about listening to you), you expect that he/she will.

"Much obliged to you for accepting my call. It's just going to include a moment or so of your time so that you can return to your bustling timetable."

You recognize they're occupied and that they will be free again very soon.

It can't damage to recall that time is cash and time can't be reused — when it's gone, it's gone. At the point when you take a financial specialist's time, you accept the estimation of that time. So be pleasant and thank individuals for giving you their time similarly as you would in the event that they gave you money.

Gain proficiency with The Advanced Opening of a Sales Call

Sadly, it can frequently be challenging to address the individual to whom you need to talk. Organizations are truly adept at introducing guards to keep salespeople at an excellent reliable ways from their directors and chiefs.

On the off chance that you can't contact the individual, even after you've had a go at calling outside ordinary working hours and took a stab at sneaking past the guard by attempting to get associated by means of somebody let down on the chain of command, you can try an audacious stunt to traverse.

THE OPENING SALES

For this to work, you need a fabulous snippet of data to give the individual the opposite finish of the telephone. Presenting yourself won't be sufficient.

The method works this way:

- Guardian: "Hi, you've arrived at ABC Enterprises."
- You: "Hi, I'd prefer to address John MacGregor."
- Guardian: "Would I be able to get some information about?"
- You: "This is Clara Davenport, from XYZ Consulting; he'll comprehend what it's about."

Tragically, this isn't totally obvious. You've never addressed John. What you're doing is compelling the issue. It won't generally work (now and again, the guard will check and instruct you to disappear – don't stress over that; it occurs). In any case, as a rule, the watchman will get you through because you sound certain and loose, and they expect that you're being honest.

Guards are individuals and typically fair, persevering individuals with something essential to take care of. Please make an effort not to consider them your foe but instead be set up to work around them on the off chance that they can't help you accomplish your goal.

Presently, now and again, they'll set you on the right track through without addressing the contact. In that case, you can utilize your standard opening, yet in the event that they move your call and they've told "John" what your identity is and that "he'll comprehend what it's about," you should have the option to get his/her consideration.

Thus, it would be best if you had that snippet of data to accomplish that.

For instance:

"Great morning John. I'm sorry to upset you, yet I was contemplating whether you'd heard that the law is changing tomorrow, and your site needs to tell guests that it utilizes treats? There's a fine of $40,000 for resistance, and I was trusting that we could assist you with fixing that issue before it turns into an issue for you."

This is a straight-up "sales pitch" as an opening. It's not the ideal approach to open sales calls; the best markets are somewhat more progressive. Nonetheless, if you need to push past the guardian, it's the perfect approach in the event that you would prefer not to acknowledge that you can't move beyond the watchman.

THE OPENING SALES

www.ingramcontent.com/pod-product-compliance
Lightning Source LLC
Chambersburg PA
CBHW070839220526
45466CB00002B/825